M000002936

THE
WANDERING
GOOSE

THE
WANDERING
GOOSE

*a modern fable
of how love goes*

HEATHER L. EARNHARDT

illustrated by FRIDA CLEMENTS

SASQUATCH BOOKS
SEATTLE

Printed in China
Published By Sasquatch Books

17 16 15 14 13   9 8 7 6 5 4 3 2 1

Editors: Susan Roxborough and Christy Cox
Project editor: Nancy W. Cortelyou
Illustration and Design: Frida Clements
Art direction: Anna Goldstein
Copy editor: Sherri Schultz
Library Of Congress Cataloging-In-Publication
Data Is Available.
ISBN: 978-1-57061-881-9

Sasquatch Books
1904 Third Avenue, Suite 710 | Seattle, WA 98101
(206) 467-4300
www.sasquatchbooks.com
custserv@sasquatchbooks.com

CREDITS:

Kobayashi Issa, "You remain with me" from Spring of My Life, And
Selected Haiku, translated by Sam Hamill. Copyright ©1997 by Sam
Hamill. Reprinted by arrangement with Shambhala Publications,
Inc., Boston, MA. www.shambhala.com

you remain with me,
old wild goose, no matter where
you roam—same autumn night

—KOBAYASHI ISSA

Dedications

Bug met Goose
one fine clear morning
in her garden.

Goose sauntered into the garden,
pushing his slender bill through
the densely growing hops.

"Hi there!
How are you, little bug?
My name is Goose.
And I love gardens."

"Well, hello to you, Goose.
My name is Bug.
And I love gardens too,"
replied Bug.

"Are you lost?
Where is your flock?" asked Bug.

"No, I'm not lost. I'm a wandering
kind of Goose. I like to travel alone
and see far and distant lands.
And I love the Ocean."

"I love the Ocean too," said Bug.

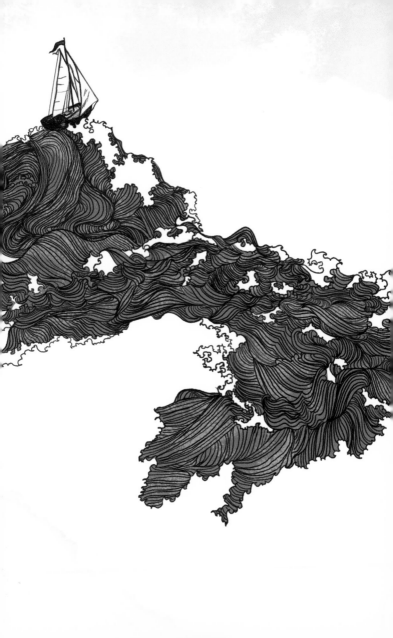

Bug and Goose became fast friends. They played all over the garden. They climbed under and over the purple coneflowers, the lupines, the sweet peas. They chewed on fresh spearmint and ate crunchy French carrots.

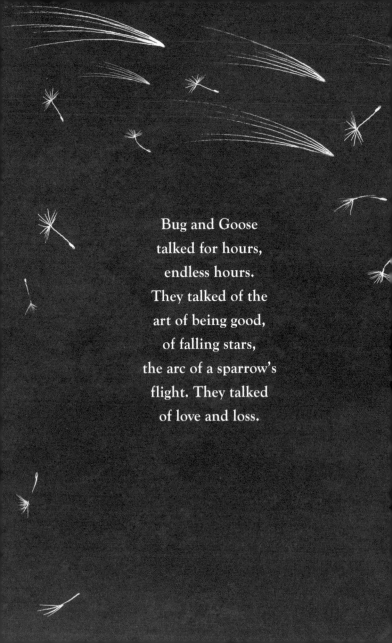

Bug and Goose
talked for hours,
endless hours.
They talked of the
art of being good,
of falling stars,
the arc of a sparrow's
flight. They talked
of love and loss.

Bug and Goose
spoke of secret things,
things that only
they could understand.
Goose whispered these
secrets in Bug's ear.

When Bug said to Goose
one fine clear morning,
"I feel as though I have been
waiting my entire life for you,"
Goose replied to her
with a poem:

WARM BOXES OF BEES
TO WARM COLD HANDS
ON FROSTY MORNINGS

When Bug said to Goose,
"Our lines, endless lines,
have brought us here together,"
Goose replied with another poem:

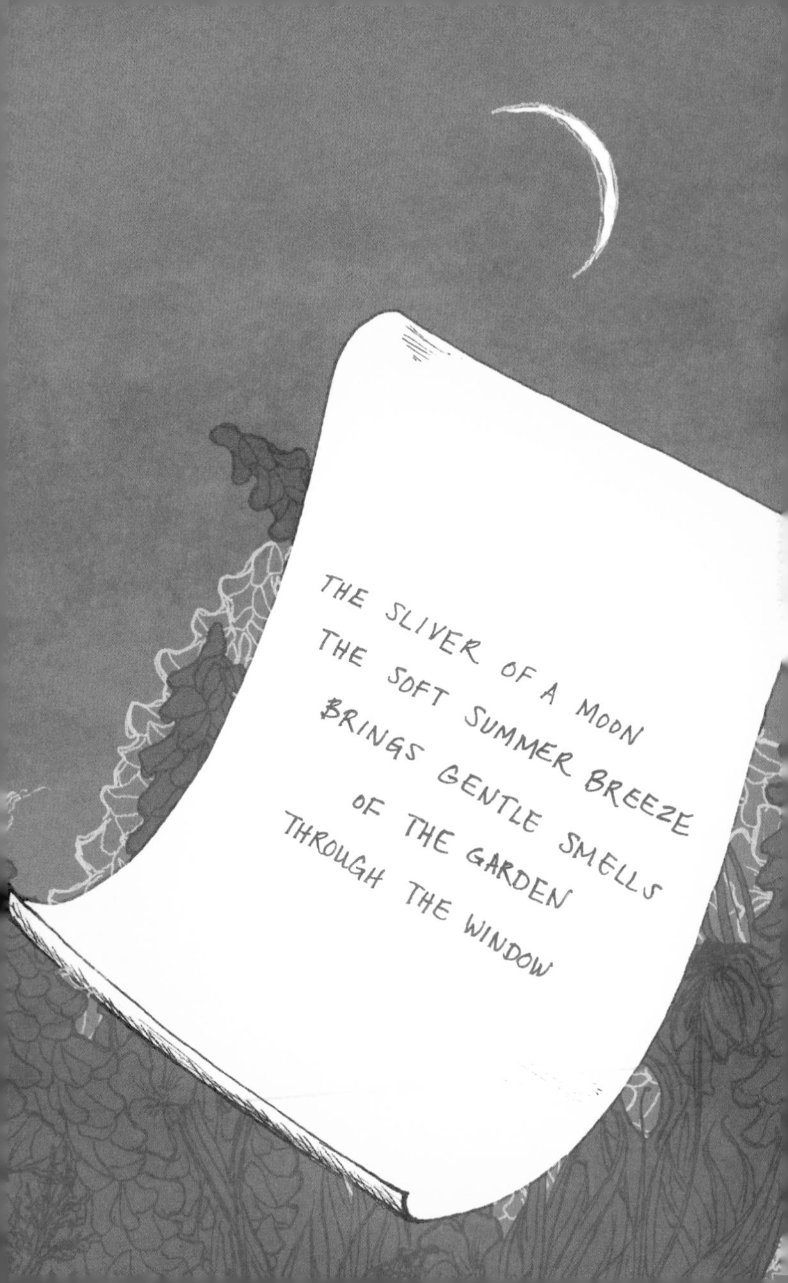

THE SLIVER OF A MOON
THE SOFT SUMMER BREEZE
BRINGS GENTLE SMELLS
OF THE GARDEN
THROUGH THE WINDOW

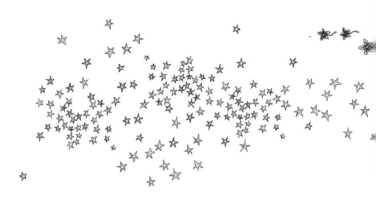

Bug and Goose played
and talked some more.
They read poetry under moonlit
skies, enjoyed long slow fires, and
danced on the rim of the well.

They watched the way the light filtered
in between the honeysuckle vines.

They made beds of stone, pillows
of milkweed, and blankets of stars.

Then
something
happened.

Bug fell in love
with Goose.
Goose fell in love
with Bug.

Bug and Goose
fell in love
with each other.

When Goose asked
Bug one fine clear
morning if they would have
loved each other ten years
ago, Bug said, "Why, yes,
Goose. Of course I would
have loved you ten years ago."
Then she thought for a
moment. "Twenty years ago,

even thirty years ago.
Of course. Of course.
And I loved you when
you were six and seven,
then nine and ten, then
twelve and twenty, and
twenty-six and thirty.
And now at thirty-four,
I still love you, Goose."

Bug and Goose
played some more.
They chased fireflies
in the evening
and played hide-and-seek
among the tall gray
sunflower stalks.

They ate thump-ripe
watermelons
and gorged themselves
on sweet greens.

After a while Bug could feel
something was not quite
right with Goose. He seemed sad.
"Goose? Are you still here?"asked Bug.

"Yes, I'm still here, Bug. But not for
long. I have to tell you something sad.
I will be leaving soon.

I must go on a new adventure.
I don't know why. But I must.
The majestic Mississippi is calling me.
Can you hear it too?"

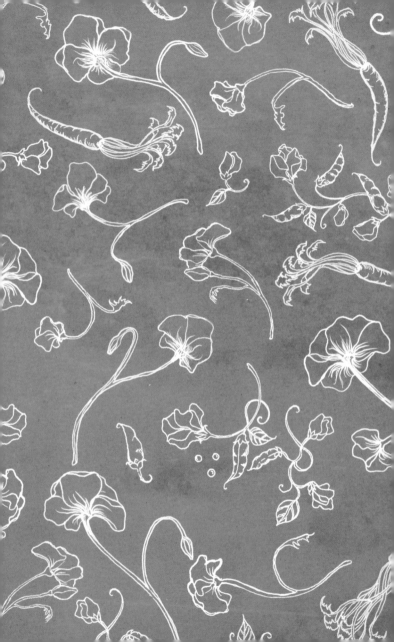

But Bug didn't hear it.
All she heard was
I,
me,
my . . .

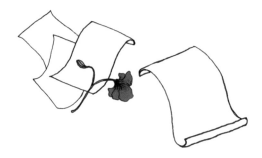

Bug and Goose continued to play and read and dance and sing and tell each other secrets. But the poetry Goose wrote to Bug was less and less. The laughter was replaced with this thing, this "I."

Then one fine clear
morning, Goose told
Bug he was leaving.

"I'm leaving now, Bug.
I will remember you.
I will always love you.
You have made your way
into this heart of mine
like a stone falling
into a clear pool."

And
then
he
was
gone.

The day Goose flew away it started to rain. It rained and rained so hard that Bug's wings were heavy and thick. So thick she couldn't fly.

It rained and rained
and rained some more.
Torrential, drunken rain.
Sharp, hurtful rain.
The clouds and the rain
pressed down on her,
pushing her down, deep
down into her red dirt.

She thought she would never
fly again. Weeks went by.
Fall gave way to winter,
winter pushed hard into
spring. Months passed.
And still it rained. Bug
dug deeper into her dirt.

Then one morning Bug awoke to the sound of a red-winged blackbird calling out. "What is he making all that noise about?" she wondered. "Can't he see I'll never fly again?" The red-winged blackbird continued to sing his song.

So Bug opened up her left eye.
Then she opened up her right eye.
She blinked. She blinked again.
And brushing away a thin
spiderweb that was caught in
her eyelashes, she saw that
the sun had finally revealed itself.

So shaking off the dust and dew from her thin but strong, oh-so strong wings, she flew, and flew, and flew. Bug stayed in her garden, her ever-changing garden, year after year. She grew new and exciting things, and met new and exciting garden friends. She had an entire flock of friends around her now. Friends who loved her.

But she never forgot about Goose.
She never forgot what they shared.
She never stopped loving him.

And on some fine clear mornings,
Bug would catch a glimpse of what she
thought was Goose, with his wrinkled
eyes still holding their secrets,
flying high in the Carolina blue sky.

ABOUT THE AUTHOR

Born in North Carolina, Heather grew up
with thick red dirt on her toes, drunken
summer thunderstorms, evening crickets,
fireflies, and food, food, and more food. Heather
owns The Wandering Goose restaurant in Seattle,
where she lives with her three children, ducks,
chickens, bees, dog, rabbit, and Bug's garden.

ABOUT THE ILLUSTRATOR

Frida Clements is an illustrator and graphic
designer known primarily for her silk-screened
concert posters. Her nature-inspired palette
complements her distinctive Scandinavian
aesthetic, in which flora and fauna are frequent
subjects. She works out of her home studio
in Seattle to the sweet sounds of her husband
composing on the piano downstairs.
She has two children.